SCHIRMER'S LIBRARY OF MUSICAL CLASSICS

Vol. 2096

Otakar Ševčík

School of Bowing Technic

(Escuela de la Técnica del Arco)

For the Violin, Op. 2
Parts 1 and 2

**Systematically and Progressively
Graded Bowing Exercises for the Violin**

Preparatory exercises. Rhythmic exercises and dividing of the bow-length. Detached and hopping styles of bowing. Exercise in sustained tones and in economizing the bow-length, i.e., holding it back as much as possible.

Edited and fingered by Philipp Mittell
English Translations by Theodore Baker
Traducción española de Lopez Miranda

ISBN 978-1-4584-2106-7

G. SCHIRMER, *Inc.*

DISTRIBUTED BY

HAL•LEONARD®
CORPORATION
7777 W. BLUEMOUND RD. P.O. BOX 13819 MILWAUKEE, WI 53213

www.schirmer.com
www.halleonard.com

CONTENTS

PART II

Pianissimo Exercises Over the Fingerboard for Developing Softness of Tone

Exercises in Arpeggios (Broken Chords) Across Three and Four Strings Using the Preceding Styles of Bowing

Employment of the Preceding Bowings in the High Positions

Abbreviations and Signs

W	Whole length of bow.
H	Half length of bow.
lH	Lower half of bow.
uH	Upper half of bow.
⅓	One-third of bow.
N	Nut of bow.
M	Middle of bow.
P	Point of bow.
M*	In the middle, then at point, then at nut.
⊓	Down-bow. [1]
V	Up-bow.
—	Broad detached stroke (détaché). [2]
•	Staccato or martellato (martelé).
'	Thrown stroke (spiccato) or saltato (sautillé).
)	Lift bow from string.

[1] When no sign appears at the beginning of an exercise, the first note is always to be taken at the nut with down-bow.

[2] Notes over which no sign for bowing is set, are to be played détaché.

Abreviaciones y Signos

W	Todo el Arco
H	Mitad del Arco
lH	Mitad inferior del Arco
uH	Mitad superior del Arco
⅓	Un tercio de Arco
N	Talón (base del Arco)
M	En el medio
P	En la punta del Arco
M*	En la mitad del Arco y de ahí hacia la punta ó hacia el talón (base del Arco)
⊓	Hacia abajo *)
V	Hacia arriba
—	Destacado largo **)
•	Staccato (picado) ó martellato (martillado)
'	Spiccato (brincado) ó Saltato (Saltillo)
)	Levantar el Arco de las cuerdas

*) De no hallarse ninguna señal al principio de un ejercicio, debe comenzarse siempre la primera nota en el talón con la arcada hacia abajo.

**) Cuando no se especifique la clase de golpe de arco, cada nota debe ser destacada.

Part I

Preparatory Exercises

No. 1

How to Hold the Bow

Practise the following with very short bows: (a) In the middle; (b) at the point; (c) at the nut. During the rests let the bow lie on the string while you count the beats aloud.

Parte I

Ejercicios Preparatorios

Nº 1

Como sostener el Arco

Trabájense los siguientes ejercicios con muy poca extensión de Arco: (a) en la mitad, (b) en la punta, (c) en el talón. Durante los silencios déjese descansar el Arco sobre las cuerdas y cuéntense los tiempos del compás en voz alta.

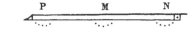

Example / Ejemplo

No. 2

How to Guide the Bow

Play the eighteen examples given below in six different ways, as shown:

Nº 2

Movimiento del Arco

Ejecútense los 18 ejemplos siguientes sin levantar el Arco, en las VI formas indicadas:

With whole bow / Todo el Arco

With half-bow / Medio Arco

In middle of bow / Con la mitad del Arco

*) First with lower half, then with upper half of the bow.

*) Primeramente con la mitad inferior y después con la mitad superior del Arco

Examples | Ejemplos

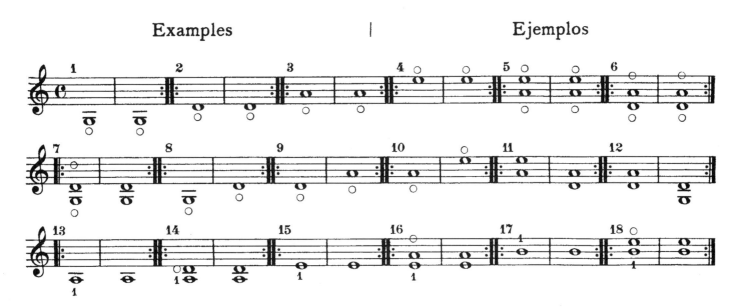

Rhythmic Exercises Whole Bows and Subdivisions of Bow	Ejercicios rítmicos y división del Arco
## No. 3	## Nº 3
Example in Whole Notes With 57 Variants	Ejemplos en redondas con 57 Variaciones
Practise each Variant of the given example from beginning to end of the latter.	Estúdiese cada variación con todo el ejemplo.

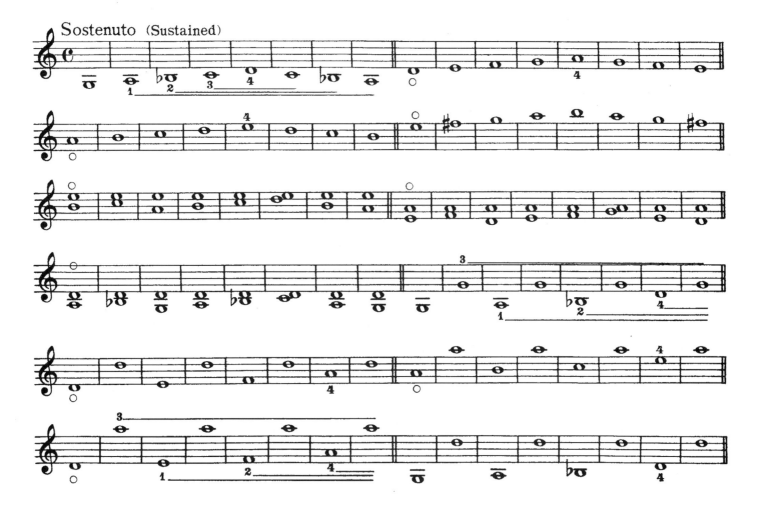

Variants
of the Preceding Example

Variaciones sobre
el ejemplo precedente

No. 4

Study in Half-Notes
with 75 Variants

Nº 4

Estudio de blancas
con 75 Variaciones

Variants

Variaciones

Whole bow
Con todo el Arco

At first with lower, then with upper half of bow
Primeramente con la mitad inferior, después con la mitad superior del Arco

Half-bow
Mitad del Arco

Whole bows and
half-bows
Todo el Arco
y mitad del Arco

The Détaché
and Springing Bow

No.5 *)

Study in Quarter-notes
With 260 Variants

In order to develop the bowing in the high positions, practise each Variant also in the 6th Position.
(See No. 8.)

Golpes de Arco
destacados y saltados

Nº 5 *)

Estudio en negras
Con 260 Variaciones

Para el desarrollo del Arco en las posiciones superiores, debe practicarse también cada variación en
la posicion 6ª (Véase Nº 8).

Syncopated
legato notes
Ligaduras sincopadas

Dotted eighth-notes
Corcheas con puntillo

14

*) Together with the bowings from 136 to 260, bowings 1 to **109 in No. 6** should be practised.

*) Simultaneamente con los estudios de golpe de arco 136 - 260 deben trabajarse también los golpes de arco 1 - 109 del Nº 6.

Viotti's style of bowing
Golpe de Arco de Viotti

Preparatory exercise
Ejercicio preparatorio

The thrown stroke
Saltado

détaché
destacado

détaché
destacado

*) This mark) shows where the bow should be lifted for the first time.

* El signo) indica donde debe levantarse el Arco la primera vez.

15

No.6

Study in Eighth-notes
With 214 Variants

For the same in the 7th Position, see No.10

Nº 6

Estudio en corcheas
con 214 cambios de Golpes de Arco

El mismo en la 7ª posición, véase Nº 10

20

Preparatory exercise
Ejercicio preparatorio

Dotted eighth-notes
Corcheas con puntillo

Syncopations
Síncopas

22

No. 7

Study in Eighth-notes, in Six-Eight Time, with 91 Bowings

For the same in the 5th Position, see No. 9.

Nº 7

Estudio en corcheas (compas $\frac{6}{8}$) con 91 cambios de golpes de Arco

El mismo en la 5ª posición, véase Nº 9.

Allegretto

Bowings
Golpes de Arco

Preparatory exercise
Ejercicio preparatorio

Dotted eighth-notes
Corcheas con puntillo

26

Employment
of the Foregoing Bowing-Exercises
in the High Positions

No. 8
With the Bowings of No. 5
6th Position

Empleo de los Ejercicios
de Arco precedentes
en las Posiciones superiores

Nº 8
Con los golpes de Arco del Nº 5
6ª Posición

6th Position
6ª Posición

No. 9
With the Bowings of No. 7
5th Position

Nº 9
Con los golpes de Arco del Nº 7
5ª Posición

5th Position
5ª Posición

IVª corda

No. 10

With the Bowings of No. 6
7th Position

Nº 10

Con los golpes de Arco del Nº 6
7ª Posición

7th Position
7ª Posición

Exercises in Arpeggios
over Three or Four Strings
Employing the Preceding
Bowing-Exercises

No. 11

With Bowings 1 to 198
in No. 6

Ejercicios de acordes arpegiados
sobre 3 y 4 cuerdas,
aplicándoseles los ejercicios
de golpes de Arco precedentes

Nº 11

Con Golpes de Arco 1 a 198
en el Nº 6

1st Position
1ª Posición

No. 12

With Bowings 1 to 198
in No. 6

Nº 12

Con Golpes de Arco 1 a 198
en el Nº 6

4th Position
4ª Posición

Part II

No. 13

Study in Triplets
With 105 Variants in the Bowing

For the same Study in the 7th position, see No.26.

Parte II

Nº 13

Estudio en Tresillos
con 105 cambios de golpes de arco

El mismo en la 7ª posición, véase Nº 26.

32

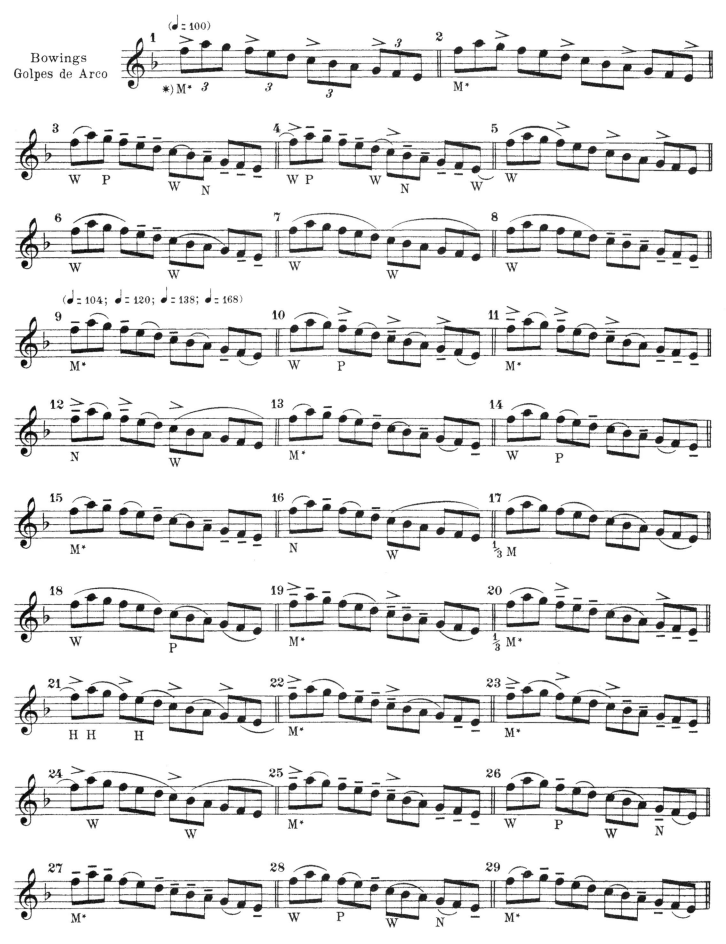

Bowings
Golpes de Arco

) All bowings marked M are to be practised in the middle of the bow, at the point, and at the nut.

) Todos los golpes de arco marcados M deben practicarse en el medio, en la punta y en el talón del arco.

No. 14

Study in Triplets (three-four time) with 77 different Bowings

For the same Study in the 4th position, see No. 25.

№ 14

Estudios en Tresillos (compás $\frac{3}{4}$) con 77 cambios de golpes de arco

El mismo estudio en la 4ª posición, véase Nº 25.

No. 15

Study in Sixteenth-Notes
(six-eight time)
with 64 different Bowings

For the same Study in the 4th position, see No.27.

Nº 15

Estudio en semicorcheas
(compás $\frac{6}{8}$)
con 64 cambios de golpes de arco

El mismo estudio en la 4ª posición, véase Nº 27.

Allegro moderato

Bowings
Golpes de Arco

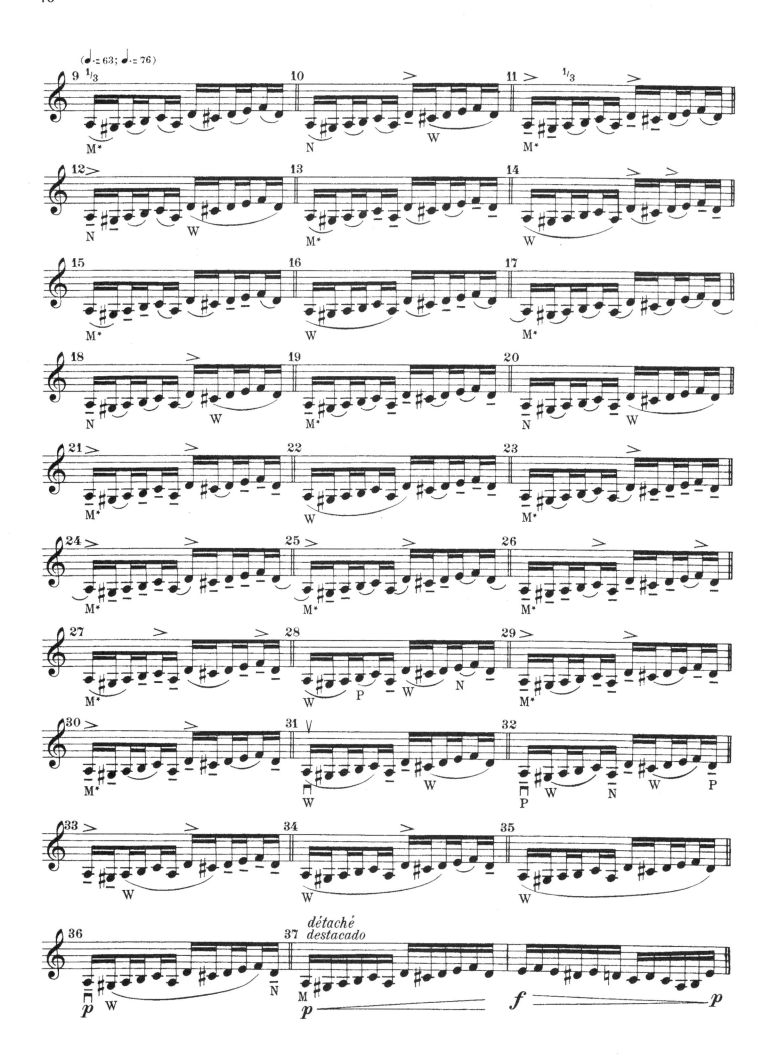

42

No.16

Study in Sixteenth-Notes
(three-four time)
with 68 different Bowings

Nº 16

Estudio en semicorcheas
(compás $\frac{3}{4}$)
con 68 cambios de golpes de arco

Allegro moderato

No. 17

Study in Sixteenth-Notes
(four-four, or common, time)
with 131 different Bowings

For the same Study in the 5th position, see No. 28.

Nº 17

Estudio en semicorcheas
(compás $\frac{4}{4}$ ó Compasillo)
con 131 cambios de golpes de arco

El mismo estudio en la 5ª posición, véase Nº 28

46

*) The second half of each measure exactly like the first. | *) La segunda mitad del compás, como la primera.

48

Dotted Sixteenths
Semicorcheas
con puntillo

Pianissimo Exercises
over the Fingerboard
For Developing Softness of Tone

No. 18

Exercise with 30 Variants

Ejercicios en *pp (pianissimo)*
sobre el Diapasón (ó Batidor)
para obtener la dulzura en el sonido

Nº 18

Ejemplo con 30 Variaciones

Variants | Variaciones

No. 19

Pianissimo Exercises
over the Fingerboard
(continued)

Exercise with 59 Variants

Nº 19

Continuación de los Ejercicios
en *pp (pianissimo)*
sobre el Diapasón (ó Batidor)

Estudio con 59 Variaciones

No. 20

Exercise
on Sustained Tones
for economizing the bow

Practise preceding Studies 3 to 7, and 13 to 17, in the following ways:

a) In groups of two measures to one bow f
b) In groups of four measures to one bow p
c) In groups of eight measures to one bow ppp

All pages referred to below are in Book I, except for exercise **14**.

Nº 20

Ejercicio en notas largas (sostenidas)
y de la retención del Arco, ejemp.
sosteniéndole de talón á punta
y vice-versa todo lo más posible

Practíquense los estudios precedentes Nº 3 á 7 y 13 a 17 en las formas siguientes:

a) en grupos de 2 compases en una sola arcada f
b) en grupos de 4 compases en una sola arcada p
c) en grupos de 8 compases en una sola arcada ppp

Las páginas á que más abajo nos referimos están todas en el Libro Iº, con excepción del ejercicio No. **14**.

See page 5 / Véase página 5

page 8 / página 8

page 11 / página 11

page 24 / página 24

page 18 / página 18

page 36
página 36

Exercises in Arpeggios
(Broken Chords)
across 3 and 4 strings,
using the preceding styles of bowing

No. 21

With Bowings 1 to 97
in No.13

Ejercicios en acordes arpegiados
sobre tres y cuatro cuerdas,
aplicándoseles los golpes
de arco precedentes

Nº 21

Con los golpes de arco
indicados en los Nᵒˢ1 á 97 del Nᵒ13

56

No. 22

With the Bowings Given in No.16

Nº 22

Con los golpes de arco del Nº16

No. 23

With the Bowings Given in No.17

Nº 23

Con los golpes de arco del Nº17

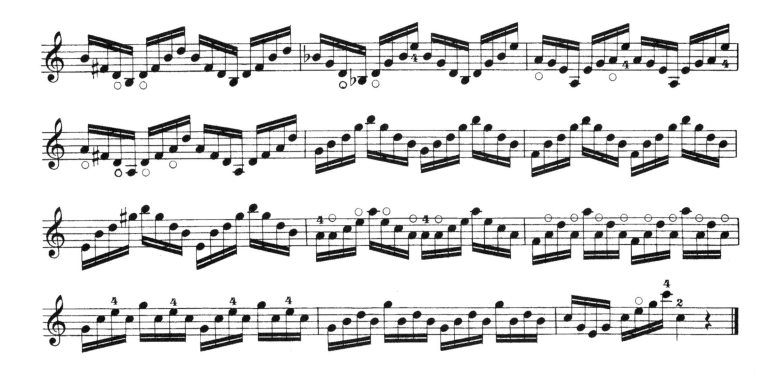

No. 24

With the Bowings Given in No.15

№ 24

Con los golpes de arco del № 15

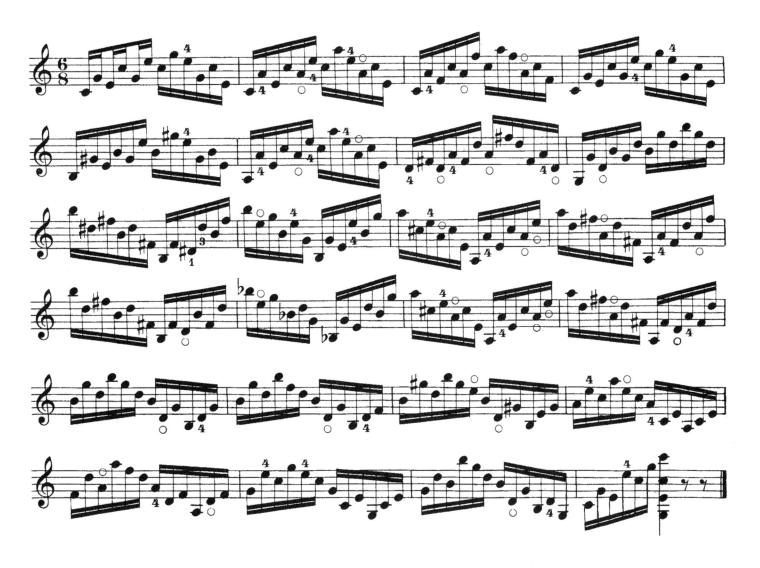

Employment of the Preceding Bowings
in the High Positions

No. 25

With the Bowings Given in No. 14

Empleo de los golpes de arco precedentes
en las posiciones superiores

Nº 25

Con los golpes de arco del Nº 14

4th Position
4ª Posición

No. 26

With the Bowings Given in No. 13

Nº 26

Con los golpes de arco del Nº 13

7th Position
7ª Posición

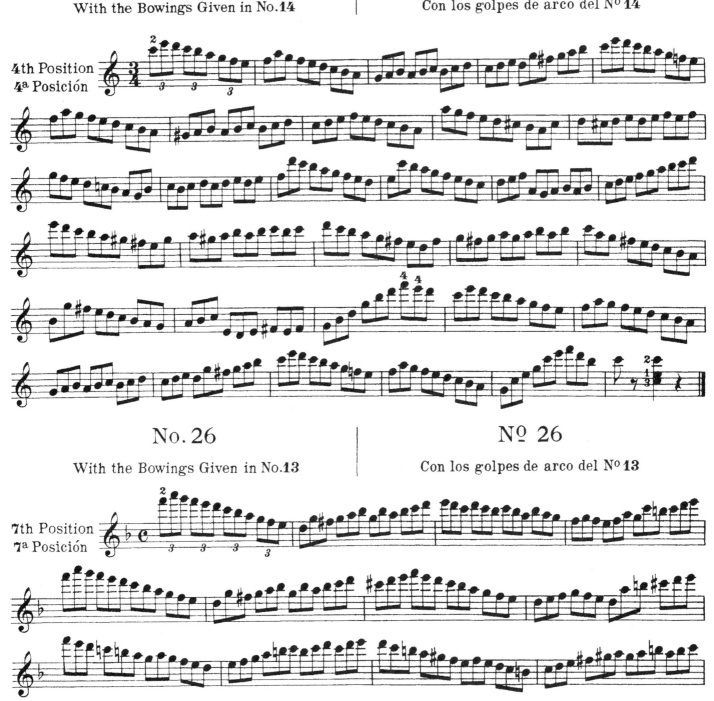

No. 27

With the Bowings Given in No.15

Nº 27

Con los golpes de arco del Nº 15

4th Position
5ª Posición

No. 28

With the Bowings Given in No.17

Nº 28

Con los golpes de arco del Nº 17

4th Position
4ª Posición

IVª corda